Charles Hudson

Abstract of the History of Lexington, Mass.

From Its First Settlement

Charles Hudson

Abstract of the History of Lexington, Mass.
From Its First Settlement

ISBN/EAN: 9783743411098

Manufactured in Europe, USA, Canada, Australia, Japa

Cover: Foto ©ninafisch / pixelio.de

Manufactured and distributed by brebook publishing software
(www.brebook.com)

Charles Hudson

Abstract of the History of Lexington, Mass.

ABSTRACT

OF THE

HISTORY OF LEXINGTON, MASS.

FROM ITS

FIRST SETTLEMENT

TO THE

CENTENNIAL ANNIVERSARY OF THE DECLARATION OF
OUR NATIONAL INDEPENDENCE.

JULY 4, 1876.

———

BY CHARLES HUDSON.

BOSTON:

PRESS OF T. R. MARVIN & SON, 40 FEDERAL STREET.

1876.

In conformity with the recommendation of Congress, the undersigned, in behalf of the citizens of Lexington, have caused the following Abstract of the HISTORY OF LEXINGTON to be prepared and published.

WEBSTER SMITH,
OTIS WENTWORTH,
ALBERT W. BRYANT,
Selectmen of Lexington.

LEXINGTON, JUNE, 1876.

HISTORICAL SKETCH.

LEXINGTON is a post town in the County of Middlesex, State of Massachusetts, situated in latitude 42° 26′ 50″ North, and longitude 70° 13′ 55″ West. It is about eleven miles West-northwest from Boston, and about fifteen miles Southeast-by-south from Lowell. It has Winchester, Woburn, and Burlington, on the Northeast; Burlington and Bedford, on the North; Lincoln, on the West; Waltham on the Southwest, and Belmont and Arlington on the Southeast. The township, like most of those in the neighborhood, is somewhat irregular in shape, and contains about twenty square miles, or about 13,000 acres. It is generally more elevated than any of the adjoining towns, unless it be Lincoln; and hence the water from Lexington runs in every direction, and finds its way to the ocean through the Shawshine, Mystic, and Charles rivers.

The hills in some parts of the town rise to a considerable height. These afford a delightful prospect, both near and remote. The soil is generally productive, and the rich peat meadows which are found in most parts of the town, add materially to the value of many farms. Lexington has been somewhat celebrated for its hay and fruit crops; but at present more particularly for its milk dairies. Some of our farmers keep from twenty to fifty, and some as high as sixty or seventy cows, making an aggregate of from 350,000 to 400,000 gallons of milk sent annually to market. Lexington has always been distinguished as a healthy town, and many invalids, on the advice of their physicians, resort to the place. It has a railroad passing directly through the centre of the town, furnishing frequent and easy communication with Boston. There is no town in the region, so near and accessible to Boston, which affords more pleasing and rural scenery than Lexington; and the Revolutionary associations are more and more attracting visitors to the place.

Lexington was formerly a part of Cambridge, and was known by the designation of "Cambridge Farms," supplying the main village with hay and wood. There was no permanent settlement at the "farms" till about 1640. The early settlers came mostly from Cambridge and Watertown, but they were at first few in number. It was not till after the close of Philip's war, that there was any considerable increase of the population. In 1670 there could not have been over eighty-five or ninety inhabitants at the "farms," but in 1690 there was probably three times that number. Among the first wants of every early New England settlement, were those of church privileges. In 1682 the settlers petitioned to be set off as a distinct precinct. The old parish of Cambridge opposing, it was not till 1691 that the Court granted the "farms" a separate corporate existence. Their first object after being made a precinct, was to provide for religious worship. They erected a meeting-house, and employed a minister before 1693. But he unfortunately died in 1697, and after some delay, in 1698, they settled John Hancock, a graduate from Harvard, a young man of good promise. He remained with his people till his death in 1752. He was a man of superior talents, and of great usefulness, and probably exerted more influence than any clergyman in the county. If a difficulty arose in any of the churches, and a Council was called, Mr. Hancock must be on the Council, where he generally became Moderator, and frequently the Council itself. In those days, when the churches were much fewer in number than at present, and ministers were usually settled for life, he gave the solemn charge to *twenty-one* ministers at their induction into office. He was as influential at home as abroad, and always managed to keep his own people united and happy. He had three sons : — First, John, who was settled a minister at Braintree, and was father of John Hancock of the Revolution; second, Thomas, a successful merchant of Boston, who adopted and educated his nephew John, who was left an orphan at the age of seven, and to whom he bequeathed his large fortune ; third, Ebenezer, who was settled as a colleague with his father, and died in 1740, after a brief ministry of six years. John Hancock the elder, built a house on what is now called Hancock Street, in Lexington, soon after his ordination in 1698, and about 1735 his son Thomas, built an addition to the house. Both the original and addition are still standing, each showing the architectural taste of the age in which it was erected, and are subjects of interest at the present day.

Mr. Hancock was succeeded in the ministry by Jonas Clarke, who was inducted into the pastoral office in 1755. He married Lucy Bowes, who was a grand-daughter of his predecessor, Rev. John Hancock. Mr. Clarke purchased and resided in the house erected by his predecessor ; so that the old building, now an object of attention, had been the ministerial mansion for more than a century. Mr. Clarke was a man of distinguished ability, and has left his mark upon his country's history. During the later years of the French and Indian wars, Mr. Clarke encouraged a warm devotion to his country, but when the English ministry first attempted to impose taxes upon the colonies, he was among the first to raise his voice against it. It was customary in those days for towns to instruct their Representatives to the General Court. When Lexington had elected their Representative, if there was any particular question before the people, he was not simply advised how to act, but he was presented with an able elaborate State paper, entering into the merits of the question, and teaching the duty of rulers and the rights and privileges of the ruled.

The Lexington Records contain a number of these valuable papers, all prepared by Mr. Clarke, which would do honor to any statesman in the country. He had a thorough knowledge of the science of civil government, and in his masterly documents he met the particular issues of the day, and showed in the clearest manner that, as English subjects, we were deprived of the rights and privileges of British freemen, which were granted to us by our charter, and confirmed by the Constitution of Great Britain ; and that, during the whole controversy, we were in the right, and Parliament in the wrong : that they, in truth, and not we, were the rebels, ignoring, disregarding, and trampling upon the fundamental principles of their own organic law. These papers not only instructed his own townsmen, but by their publication they enlightened the public mind and prepared the people, not simply to resist the encroachments of Great Britain, but to establish free institutions, and to perform all the duties of Republican citizens. Mr. Clarke possessed a clear, vigorous, and well-balanced mind, and was always exercised by high moral principles, whether acting the divine or the statesman. He was, in fact, religiously political and politically religious, and was progressive and conservative at the same time. He was the friend, adviser and compeer of Adams, Hancock, and Warren, who frequently found a home under his roof and wise instruction from his counsel.

Lexington was peculiarly fortunate in being favored by two such clergymen as Hancock and Clarke, whose united ministry exceeded a century, and whose wisdom guided the people in the arts of peace and in the perils of war. Their lives, their teaching, and their characters, were so blended with the affairs of the town, that they are as necessarily a part of the history of Lexington, as Washington is of the American Revolution.

But Lexington has a civil and a military, as well as an ecclesiastic history. Lexington was made a precinct in 1691, but incorporated as a town in 1713. As a municipal corporation they laid out highways, provided for the support of the poor, and established that indispensable institution of New England, *free schools*. The town being exclusively agricultural, and lying near the neighborhood of manufactures and commerce, their young men, too frequently, have been induced to leave Lexington, and hence the increase of population has been very gradual. And this natural growth received a further check in 1754, when a thousand acres of their territory, with the inhabitants thereon, were taken from them to help form the town of Lincoln.

But Lexington has a military history which reflects no dishonor upon the place. In the French and Indian war Lexington acted no insignificant part. From 1755 to 1763, taking the number of men in each year will give a total of one hundred and fifty men, who were found on every battle-field — at Louisburg, Quebec, Crown Point, Ticonderoga, Fort William-Henry, and wherever a foe was to be encountered or a daring deed to be performed. Some of the Lexington men were attached to the famous corps known as " Rogers' Rangers," a corps in which Stark served his military apprenticeship; a corps whose *name* was expressive of the life they led, *ranging* through the wilderness, seeking their wary savage foe by day and by night, in silent glens or secret ambush ; a corps whose winter quarters were in tedious marchings amid drifted snows and ice-clad hills, relying sometimes upon snow-shoes and sometimes upon skates for locomotion, and carrying their only arsenal and commissariat in their packs. In such a corps were some of the hardy sons of Lexington trained, they knowing that their lives were in their own hands, and that their escape from the tomahawk and scalping knife, the tortures of the fagot or ignominious slavery, depended entirely upon their own severe trials, perpetual watchings, and determined courage. The further military history of Lexington will appear hereafter.

We have already alluded to the controversy of the Colony with the mother country. This was continuous from the passage of the *Stamp Act* in 1765 to the opening of the Revolution. This controversy, which excited the attention of every town and village, was in no place better understood than in Lexington. The clear and elaborate instruction of parson Clarke, the frequent visits of Hancock and Adams, kept these questions constantly before the people ; and the whole subject was discussed, not merely in a declamatory and passionate way, but on its real merits. So that when our fathers resorted to arms, they rallied not as an ignorant, infuriated mob, but as a band of patriots, knowing their rights, and resolved to resist unjust oppression.

After pouring out their blood and treasure in the cause of Great Britain, in subduing the enemy in Canada, the people of the Colony flattered themselves that they should be permitted to rest in peace, and recover from their exhaustion in the royal cause. In this expectation the people of Lexington participated. They had served faithfully in his Majesty's cause, and, feeling oppressed by impositions already made, and others in prospect, they had united with their fellow citizens in other towns, in urgent petition for relief, and earnest but humble remonstrance against these acts of oppression. But finding all such measures fruitless, they felt called upon by every patriotic consideration, and even by the sacred obligations of religion, to assert their manhood, vindicate the rights implanted by their Creator, and to hand these rights and privileges down to their posterity. They had, therefore, prepared themselves to meet the crisis whenever it should come, or whatever form it should assume. Whatever others might do, the citizens of Lexington stood firm. In 1773, two years before the breaking out of hostilities, when pretended patriots, even in Boston, faltered, Lexington gave them this assurance : — " We trust in God that, should the state of affairs require it, we shall be ready to sacrifice our estates and every thing

dear in life, yea, and life itself, in support of the common cause."
Nor was this an empty boast! When their affairs did require it,
they made the first offering in freedom's sacred cause.

But the good people of Lexington did not rely upon declarations
alone. They made all the preparation their limited means would
allow, to supply themselves with the munitions of war. They voted
"To provide a suitable quantity of flints," "to bring two pieces of
cannon from Watertown and mount them," "to provide a pair of
drums for the use of the military company in town," "to provide
bayonets at the town's cost, for one-third of the training soldiers,"
"to have the militia and alarm list meet for a view of their arms," &c.
And that these votes should not prove a mere dead letter, commit-
tees were chosen to carry them into effect; all of which showed that
the people were in earnest, and expected that war would ensue.

It is due to the patriots of Lexington and our fathers generally, to
correct an error which has prevailed extensively, that they took up
arms rather than pay a *three-penny* tax upon tea. This is a narrow
view of the subject. They did object to taxation, while having no
representation in Parliament. But the claim of Great Britain was
not limited to taxation. They claimed the right of legislating for us
in "*all cases whatsoever*,"—a right to deprive us of all our civil privileges, such as the right of trial by jury, of suffrage, of taking or hold-
ing property,—a doctrine by which they could compel us to serve in
their army or navy, and fight their battles in any part of the world,
—in a word, the right to make us slaves. And in fact, before we
took up arms, their Parliament reduced some of these principles to
practice. Their act changing the Charter of Massachusetts, practically deprived us of trial by jury, and of other domestic rights and
immunities which we all held dear, and was their first bold step of
exercising absolute control over the Colonies. They had passed
such laws, and had sent a Governor, backed by military power, to
enforce them. The resolution, on their part, was made,—the
purpose was fixed. Their law should be executed, even at the point
of the bayonet.

Nor were the Colonists undecided. Old Middlesex had been in
council, and from a full view of the subject they say:—"Life and
death, or what is more, freedom or slavery are, in a peculiar sense,
now before us; and the choice and success, under God, depend
greatly upon ourselves." And after asserting that the law was

unconstitutional and ought not to be obeyed, they add, "No danger shall affright, no difficulties shall intimidate us ; and if in support of our rights, we are called upon to encounter death, we are yet undaunted, sensible that he can never die too soon who lays down his life in support of the laws and liberties of his country." Such was the resolution and sentiment of the county. And Lexington was not a whit behind the foremost in this patriotic self-devotion. In fact its citizens, two years before, had announced to their fellow sufferers their trust in God that they should be ready to sacrifice fortune and life in the common cause, whenever the crisis should require it. The people were also sustained by the policy of the Provincial Congress, which had ordered the organization of minute-men, appointed general officers, and practically made the Chairman of the Committee of Safety, Commander-in-Chief of all the military force of the Province. They had also, in a moral sense, ordered disobedience to the late laws of Parliament : but directed the people to refrain from direct acts of war, and "not fire unless fired upon." The issue was practically made up, and nothing was wanting but an occasion to try the same. And the few military stores at Concord furnished an opportunity to test the spirit of the people.

THE BATTLE OF LEXINGTON.

The Spring of 1775 opened with strong indications that some military demonstration by General Gage was about to be made. The state of things at that period was this : Gage was in Boston with about three thousand men, who were wearied with inaction, and anxious for an opportunity to display their prowess in the field. Colonel Leslie had been sent to Salem to destroy some stores, but the expedition was abortive. Two British officers in disguise had been sent to Worcester and to Concord, where a few military stores were collected, to spy out the land, ascertain the location of the stores, and the most feasible approach to the respective towns. General Gage had been accused at home of inactivity, and he knew that Generals Howe, Clinton, and Burgoyne were soon to join and probably supersede him. The ministry and Gage had concurred in the policy of seizing Hancock and Adams, and sending them to England for trial. All these facts would naturally prompt the royal Governor to action.

2

On the other hand, the patriots were not inactive or blind to these indications. Hancock, as President of the Provincial Congress, had important duties to perform, and great responsibility to incur ; and as Chairman of the Committee of Safety, he was practically the Chief Magistrate of the Province, and the Commander-in-Chief of her troops. And Samuel Adams, who exerted more influence in the Province than any other man, was devising measures to prepare the people for self-government, and instructing them in the best means of attaining that rich blessing ; while Warren and other vigilant patriots were watching the actions of Gage, and concerting signals by which his movements might be heralded to their friends in the country. It seemed obvious to the whole community that Gage had his eye upon Hancock and Adams, who were sojourning in Lexington with their friend and compeer, Rev. Jonas Clarke, whose teachings had fully impressed his people with their rights and duties as citizens. The patriots were aware that the few stores collected at Concord had attracted the Governor's attention, and measures were adopted to ensure their safety. Such was the outward appearance of things on the morning of the 19th of April, 1775.

On the previous day some twelve or fifteen British officers were detailed to pass over the different roads leading to Concord, to intercept all travellers, and to return late at night, as is believed, and seize Hancock and Adams, known to be at Lexington. To remove all suspicion, these officers were to dine at Cambridge, and so be thus far on their midnight expedition. Other precautions were taken by the Governor to avoid suspicion. The troops selected for the expedition were removed from the main body on the pretence of being taught some new evolution and drill. Boats from the ships in the stream were collected, for the ostensible purpose of having them painted, but really to transport the troops across the river.

Believing that these arrangements had secured perfect secrecy, about eleven o'clock at night, the command under Colonel Smith was safely landed on Cambridge shore, near where the present Court House stands. The evening was propitious, and Gage flattered himself that he had eluded the vigilance of his watchful enemies, when, to his surprise, he was informed that the departure and destination of the troops were known. To avoid any spread of this intelligence, he ordered sentinels to be posted forthwith, in all suitable places, to see that no person be permitted to leave the town that night. But the bird had flown. Warren, ever watchful in freedom's cause, had sent Paul Revere by way of Charlestown, and William Dawes by way of the Neck, to convey the intelligence of the movement to Hancock and Adams at Lexington. Thus, while Smith's command were marching, or rather wading stealthily through the marshes in Cambridge, these messengers were spreading the alarm, and the lantern at the old North (Christ) Church was, with the velocity of light, conveying the tidings of the march, and, by inference, the destination of the troops, in every direction. Smith had not moved far before the church bells and the alarm guns taught him that his movement was known, and that danger was impending. He consequently sent back for a re-enforcement, and at the same time ordered Pitcairn, with the light troops, to proceed with the utmost despatch to Concord, and take possession of the bridges.

Meantime, the people of Lexington had taken the alarm. The passing of the British officers up the road at a late hour of the day, created a suspicion that they had a design upon Hancock and Adams ; and a sergeant's guard was stationed at Clarke's house, where the patriots had their temporary abode. But when Revere arrived about midnight with the intelligence that a large force, supposed at that time to be an entire brigade, had left Boston, destined, in all probability, for Lexington and Concord, Captain Parker, commanding the Lexington minute-men, summoned them to meet forthwith at their usual place of parade. Obeying readily, they were paraded on the Common between one and two o'clock, when they were ordered to load their pieces with balls, but "not fire unless they were fired upon." The night being chilly, and no further intelligence of the approach of the British troops being received, the company at about two o'clock were dismissed to reassemble at the ringing of the bell, beating of the drum, and the firing of the alarm guns. The first certain intelligence they had of the approach of the troops, was that they were near by, marching rapidly upon the town. The bell rang, the alarm guns proclaimed the approach, and the drums beat to arms. The men, who had been dismissed, were scattered about the village. Some had gone to their respective homes, others who lived at a distance, had repaired to Buckman's tavern, hard by, and upon the alarm they rushed to the parade ground in haste.

But not more than fifty had reached the spot, when the rash and impetuous Pitcairn, at the head of his troops, rushed upon them with a shout, denouncing them as rebels, and with an oath commanding them to throw down their arms and disperse. The little band, realizing that they were standing upon their own ground, where they were wont to assemble, manfully retained their position; a volley of blank cartridges was fired, but the Provincials stood firm. Enraged at this, Pitcairn discharged his pistol, and ordered the whole platoon to fire. A fatal volley ensued, which decimated the patriot line. Several of the Provincials returned the fire on the spot. Captain Parker, seeing the folly of confronting eight hundred regular troops with fifty undisciplined militia, ordered his men to disperse, which order they obeyed, several of them returning the fire as they left the Common. The British pursued the retreating patriots, and two were shot down as they were leaving or had left the green. One or more British soldiers were wounded by the return fire, and Pitcairn's horse was struck in two places.*

Here let us pause for a moment! Fifty undisciplined yeomanry stood up manfully in the face of eight hundred veteran troops, and would not disperse at their bidding, and returned the fire when fired upon! A Spartan steadfastness rarely equalled. This was truly *organized* resistance, both morally and legally. The Provincials had resolved in Congress, in conventions, in town meetings, and in all private gatherings, that they would resist if the British should attempt to enforce their oppressive laws by military force, but would not fire unless they were fired upon. This was morally an organized principle, well understood and controlling. The Lexington men were also organized *legally*. The company of minute-men were organized agreeably to the order of the Provincial Congress; Parker was their lawful commander, who had summoned his company together in consequence of the approach of the king's troops, and ordered them to load their pieces with powder and ball; he paraded them in the very face of the king's troops, which were rapidly approaching, bound on a hostile expedition. And all this took place under the eye and with the approbation of John Hancock, who, as

---

* Though some of our friends, jealous of the honors of Lexington, have pretended to doubt whether Lexington men returned the fire in the morning, John Munroe, Ebenezer Munroe, Benjamin Sampson, William Tidd, Nathaniel Munroe, and Solomon Brown, who were present on the occasion, testify to the fact of their firing. Dr. Warren, John Hancock, and others, were appointed by the Provincial Congress on the 12th of June, 1775, to inquire into the matter, and they reported that the British fired and killed eight men, and that the *fire was returned by some of the survivors*. Parson Clarke says the same. Gordon, Bancroft, and Frothingham, admit the firing. The British account at the time, admits that one British soldier was wounded, and Pitcairn's horse hit twice.

Chairman of the Committee of Safety, was virtually Commander-in-Chief of the military, and who would have come upon the Common and assumed the command, but for the remonstrance of Adams and Clarke. Surely, here was organized resistance, such as would constitute treason by the British law,—an organization as perfect, nay, more perfect, than existed at Concord or any place upon the line, till General Heath took the command. At Lexington the Provincials acted under the eye of the Commander-in-Chief, but no where else upon the line.

The men on Lexington Common practically acted under orders which were well understood, when they returned the British fire. The soldier, when placed on picket or employed as a skirmisher, expects no superior by his side to tell him when to fire. He acts on general principles, and knows that the very position in which he is placed must, in most cases, preclude the idea of a superior to give him verbal orders. So the members of Capt. Parker's Company acted on the same principle; and when they were ordered not to fire until they were fired upon, they knew when that contingency occurred, they had full authority to fire. Soon after the British had left for Concord, a number of their soldiers who had straggled from the main body were discovered, and six of them were made prisoners, and sent to Burlington for safe-keeping. This was certainly an act of *military, physical resistance*—and these were the first prisoners made in the Revolution.

The British, after halting on Lexington Common, firing a salute, and giving three cheers in honor of their supposed victory, marched direct for Concord, where the intelligence of their firing upon and killing six or eight of Lexington men, had preceded them, as appears by the deposition of Captain Barrett and fifteen others of Concord. The militia from several towns, who had collected at the village of Concord, knowing that the British had fired upon the militia at Lexington and killed several of their members, when they saw them approaching in martial array, retreated to the highlands north of the village, west of the river. Smith, on his arrival at Concord, detailed Captain Parsons with a hundred men to destroy the stores intrusted to the care of Colonel Barrett. Captain Laurie, with about the same number of men, was posted at the North bridge, to secure the safe return of Captain Parsons; while Smith, with the main body of the troops, remained in the village, to destroy what stores they could find there.

In his wanton destruction of the few articles he found in the centre of the town, fire was communicated to the Court House and several other buildings, which led the Provincials on the hill which overlooked the centre, to fear that the whole village would be laid in ashes, and they resolved to march to the scene of danger to stay the flames. But there was a lion in the way: Laurie, with his one hundred men, guarded the bridge over which they must pass. The Americans on the hill had now increased to about four hundred and fifty, and the passage from the hill to the bridge was by a narrow causeway over wet and swampy ground, so that the approach to the bridge would expose the front to the direct fire of those who guarded the bridge. Who, then, would occupy this dangerous position, this post of honor? The Americans were paraded in a line upon the hill. The Concord companies, two in number, ranked the others, and so occupied the right, which rested on the road which led to the bridge. Captain Davis, with his Acton minute-men, occupied a position in a central part of the line. They were paraded in the same order they had adopted at a muster a short time before, when the question of position was decided.

But it would seem that there was a little hesitancy in assuming the right, and so leading the column to the bridge. The officers held a consultation. What occurred in that conference, we learn only by what followed. When the consultation closed, Captain Davis of the Acton minute-men, advanced to his company in a central part of the line, and drawing his sword, said, with emotion : " There is not a man in my company that's afraid to go," and, wheeling them out of their position in the line, marched to the right of the line to lead the Provincials over the causeway, the real point of danger, to dislodge the British. That there was some delicacy about occupying this post of danger is apparent from the further acknowledged fact that Captain Smith of Lincoln, to whom the honor of the right did not belong, offered to place his company in that position.

When the column was ready to move, Major Buttrick of Concord assumed the command, and led the column to the bridge. Colonel Robinson of Westford, an officer, but of another regiment, volunteered to attend him. As they approached the bridge, they were fired upon by the British. The first guns, only two or three in number, did no execution, the balls, probably by design, striking the water. Then followed a few scattering shots, one of which wounded

Luther Blanchard, a fifer in the Acton company. These were succeeded by a volley, by which Captain Davis and Abner Hosmer, both of Acton, were killed. On seeing this, Major Buttrick, prompted by the sentiment which actuated the whole community, ordered his men to fire. The order was promptly obeyed, killing one and wounding six or eight of the enemy. The British immediately retreated in haste and confusion towards the village, and were soon met by a re-enforcement, when they all fell back upon the main body near the meeting house. The Americans pursued them over the bridge, where one of the wounded British soldiers was cruelly killed by a hatchet, as he was struggling to rise from the ground, — an act unauthorized, and condemned by all in command. A part of the Americans, after crossing the bridge, turned off to the left and ascended the hill east of the main road, while another portion returned to the highlands whence they came, bearing the remains of Davis and Hosmer. Military order was now broken up, and the militia were unwisely permitted to scatter to obtain their breakfast. In the meantime the detail sent to Colonel Barrett's to destroy the stores, returned, passed the bridge, and joined the main body unmolested ; though Bancroft and Frothingham both say it might easily have been cut off.

The British met with but partial success in destroying military stores. The delay at Lexington and the alarm that preceded them, enabled Colonel Barrett to conceal most of the stores, so that the British found only a few gun carriages and articles of but little value. After the affair at the North bridge, which consisted in exchanging two or three volleys, and which lasted but a few minutes, everything remained quiet till the enemy left Concord. The fall of Captain Davis seems to have extinguished the military ardor of the Provincials. Two hours were suffered to pass without any action being taken or measures adopted. The British were equally inactive, till about twelve o'clock, when they commenced their retreat. The main body moved on the direct road toward Lexington, while a strong flank guard marched over the hill which commanded the road. When the main body of the British passed Merriam's Corner, where the hill terminates, the flank guard came into the main road, and seeing the men from Reading, Billerica, and Bedford, coming down the road which would intersect their line of march they halted, faced about, and fired upon them. The Provincials at once returned the fire, killing two of the British. This was the signal for a gener conflict. Here, in fact, the *battle proper* commenced — not at t north bridge, — but near the junction of the Bedford and Lexingt roads, nearly two miles from the North bridge. The affair at t bridge was a mere skirmish, where the British had but one hundr men present, and where but two or three volleys were fired ; b here the whole British force was united, and the firing becan general on both sides.

The Provincials rallied ; men came in from Reading and oth towns on the the north, the Sudbury men and others from the sout and with those who had been in the town in the early part of t day, all joined in the attack. Smith found himself assailed every hand. He attempted to arrest their pursuit by presenting h whole force, but he soon saw that this was only exposing his men shots from trees, and walls and thickets. He threw out his fla guard, but the Provincials out-flanked the flankers. A large co pany from Woburn, led by Loammi Baldwin, met the British in Li coln, and did good service ; and Captain Parker had rallied his mu lated company, and appeared in the field to avenge the brutality the morning. In passing the woody defiles in Lincoln the Briti suffered severely. They attempted to resist, but where was the fo They had recourse to the bayonet, but they charged in empty a They soon found that their safety was in flight. They did, ho ever, attempt to make one formal stand. Just after they enter Lexington, near the old Viles Tavern, Smith posted a detail of h men upon a rocky bluff by the side of the road, to hold the pursue in check, while he should rally his fugitives on what is known Fiske Hill. Taking advantage of the woods and a narrow defile, brought his troops to a stand, and attempted to form a line whe he could, temporarily at least, hold the Provincials in check. B before his line was fully formed, his rear, stationed on the blu was driven in upon his half-formed column, creating great confusio In the mean time a considerable number of the Provincials, avoidir the troops on the bluff, had passed through the woods and secrete themselves behind a lot of split rails by the side of the road whe Smith was attempting to form his men ; and when his rear w driven in, and the Americans were gathering around him and pic ing off his men, the Provincials from their hiding place behind t rails poured a well-directed, enfilading fire into his ranks, creatii perfect confusion and dismay. Here Smith was severely wounded, and Pitcairn also was wounded and thrown from his horse, which in his sudden flight bounded from the road, and with all his trappings became an easy prey to the pursuers. The horse with the accoutrements was sent to Concord, where they were sold at auction. Captain Nathan Barrett purchased the holsters and the pistols, marked with Pitcairn's name, and offered them to General Washington, who declined them. They were afterwards presented to General Putnam, who carried them through the remainder of his active service in the war. They descended in the family, and became the property of his grand-son, John P. Putnam, of Cambridge, New York. They are now the property of his widow.

Another incident occurred at Fiske Hill, worthy of note. We have already seen that the Acton men were the first to attack, and we may add, foremost in the pursuit : — James Heywood, one of Acton's proud sons, a young man of twenty-two years, being one of the foremost in pressing upon the enemy, at the easterly foot of Fiske Hill came in contact with a British soldier who had stopped to slake his thirst at a well. The Briton presented his musket, and said defiantly, " *You are a dead man.*" " *And so are you,*" retorted young Heywood. They both fired and both fell ; the Briton dead, and Heywood mortally wounded.

After the affair on Fiske Hill, where Smith was wounded, he made no further attempt to check the pursuers. By their own confession " they were driven like sheep," and were so exhausted that, when they met their re-enforcement, they " threw themselves upon the ground with their tongues running out of their mouths, like dogs after a chase." The same force which passed Lexington village so proudly in the morning, returned a perfect rabble rout in the afternoon, seeking safety in their flight.

The re-enforcement for which Smith called the night before, did not leave Boston till about nine o'clock that morning, and coming out through Roxbury, did not meet the fugitives till nearly two. This force, commanded by Lord Percy, consisted of about eleven hundred men, with two pieces of artillery. He met Smith on the plain about half a mile below Lexington Common, and planted one of his field pieces on a mound where the present High School house stands, and the other on the swell of land in the rear of the house recently erected by Mr. Levi Prosser. With these he kept the Provincials

•   3

at bay, while he gave temporary rest to the flying troops he came to protect. Wherever he saw a collection or group of men, he opened upon them with one of his field pieces, and by dispersing them gave rest to the British troops. Several shots were thrown into the village, one of which struck the church, and passing out of the pulpit window, lodged in the northerly part of the Common. This timely relief saved Smith's detachment from utter ruin. It has been a credited tradition that, before reaching the re-enforcement, and not knowing when or where relief would reach them, Smith would have surrendered, if his pursuers had had any commanding officer to whom he could have delivered his sword. But Percy gave him temporary relief, and enabled his men to take a little rest and refreshment, privileges which they greatly abused. And to the dishonor of Percy it may be said, that the lawlessness and vandalism of the troops, which took place under his eye, and which, as commanding officer, he could have prevented, he appears to have allowed without restraint. They entered the houses on the plain, and not only demanded food, which was readily given them, but they commenced a system of pillage, and even a wanton destruction of property, ending in burning the houses they had plundered.

While the British were resting at Lexington, General Heath, who had been appointed by the Provincial Congress one of the Major Generals, to command any troops that were called out, came over from Watertown and assumed the command of the Americans, and controlled their movements in a measure, the rest of the day. He was attended by Dr. Warren, who rendered important service during the retreat ; he was seen in the hottest of the battle, encouraging the men, and had a hair-pin shot from his ear-lock by a British ball.

Percy, as senior officer, took command of the king's troops, and commenced his retreat. It was nearly three o'clock when he left Lexington. He undoubtedly felt secure, as there appeared to be no new gathering of Provincials to annoy his flanks, and he relied upon his cannon to protect his rear. But while he was reposing at Lexington, the militia were collecting at Arlington from Watertown, Needham, Dedham and other towns on the south, and from Beverly, Salem and Lynn on the north ; and the gallant men of Danvers who marched *sixteen miles in four hours*, were on the ground to oppose his retreat. And when he had passed the defiles and entered upon the open land in Arlington, he found the Provincials ready to annoy him, and even to dispute his passage. He found that every tree was a fortress and every wall a rampart. He threw out his flank guards, but many of them were picked off by unseen foes, and the progress of his march only brought him in contact with increased numbers of his enemies. And while he was thus annoyed in flank and opposed in front, the troops which had pursued him from Lexington hung upon his rear, inflicting severe damage. The British became desperate, assailing the old and defenceless, murdering non-combatants, abusing women and children, and setting fire to houses occupied by the sick, who were compelled to crawl from their dwellings to escape the ravages of the flames. But this wanton barbarity only increased the boldness and indignation of the pursuers. Heath and Warren breathed new life and energy into the Americans, and led them in direct attack. Percy became sensible of his danger, and had recourse to his artillery, but his cannon had lost their terror. He found himself pressed on every hand. The roads before him were guarded; the rocks, trees and fences were manned on every side ; and while he was exposed to this unseen foe, and his men were falling by shots from hidden marksmen, others, more bold and desperate, approached him in the open field, and poured well-directed volleys into his ranks. Percy found himself in the same plight that Smith was, whom he met in Lexington, and saw that nothing could save him but flight. He therefore made a desperate effort to seek the protection of the ships. The British were closely pressed. Heath directed the movements of the militia, and Warren nerved their hearts ; so that, under a galling fire, Percy spent his energies in speed, being more anxious to gain the protection of friends, than to encounter pursuing foes. When he was entering upon Charlestown Neck, as the sun was about withdrawing its light from the revolting scene of blood and carnage, General Heath, fearing for the safety of Charlestown, if he pursued Percy any further, called off his men, and suffered the weary fugitives to seek repose under the cover of their ships.

The suffering of the British soldiers, especially those who went to Concord, must have been extremely severe. The length of the march, the rapidity of their movement, the want of refreshment, the burden of their wounded, the extreme heat of the day, and the vigorous press of the pursuers, must have taxed their endurance to an excessive degree, and taught them the danger of invading the rights of freemen.

While the events of the day do not present any of those desperate charges or collisions of arms which often occur in a pitched battle, there are displays of cool, collected courage, of self-sacrificing devotion to principle, of individual heroism, which will compare with the brightest examples in Greek or Roman history. The case of Dr. Downer, of West Cambridge, in which he encountered a British regular, and after a desperate struggle, transfixed him on his bayonet, was a deed of noble daring. We can hardly conceive of a more trying position than that in which the minute-men of Lexington were placed on the 19th of April, 1775. To stand unmoved in the presence of vastly superior numbers rushing upon them in battle array, requires more than ordinary moral courage. And in this particular case there were circumstances which heightened this display of cool intrepidity. War had not been declared or hostilities commenced; and the men on the field knew that they were not only exposed to British bullets, but to a British halter, if they stood together with arms in their hands, and refused to disperse at the order of the king's officers, clothed with royal authority. But still they were undaunted. Those already upon the field stood firm, and those who were a little later walked to the field and paraded in the very face of the British regulars, who were rushing upon the Common with a defiant shout.

The minute-men were ordered to disperse by Pitcairn, but they heeded not the command. A British volley was fired, and the command to lay down their arms and disperse was repeated with an oath and a pistol shot, but they stood undaunted. And it was not till the fatal volley had decimated their little band, that they left the field at the command of Captain Parker. Their situation was more critical, more trying, than that of any men that day. The men who led the attack at the North bridge, and those who pursued the British that day, were truly courageous; but they all had the stimulating fact that the British commenced the slaughter at Lexington, to fire their bosoms and to urge them upon the foe. Courage, like other passions or qualities of the mind, is increased or depressed by outward circumstances; and it requires more true moral courage to stand fearless and unmoved, as did the minute-men of Lexington in the morning, than to join in pursuit, or even march to the attack, after hostilities have commenced and numbers are pressing to your support.

But Lexington furnished individual cases of bravery, which merit special notice. Jedediah Munroe was wounded in the morning, but as soon as his wound in the arm could be dressed, he mounted his horse and rode to an adjoining town, spreading the alarm, and rallying the citizens. He returned, joined the company, and was killed in the afternoon. " History, Roman history," says Everett in his Lexington address, "does not furnish an example of bravery that outshines that of Jonas Parker. A truer heart did not bleed at Thermopylæ. He was next door neighbor to Mr. Clarke, and had evidently imbibed a double portion of his lofty spirit. Parker was often heard to say that, be the consequences what they might, and let others do what they pleased, he would never run from the enemy. He was as good as his word — better. Having loaded his musket, he placed his hat containing his amunition, on the ground between his feet, in readiness for the second charge. At the second fire from the enemy he was wounded and sunk upon his knees, and in this condition discharged his gun. While loading it again upon his knees, and striving in the agonies of death to redeem his pledge, he was transfixed by a bayonet, and thus died on the spot where he first stood and fell." We might mention other examples of individual bravery, but our limits will not permit.

The Americans lost on that fatal day forty-nine killed, thirty-nine wounded, and five missing. Lexington lost ten killed, and ten wounded, nearly one-fourth of the whole number. The Lexington killed were Robert Munroe, who had been standard-bearer in the king's service in the French war, Jonas Parker, Samuel Hadley, Jonathan Harrington, Jr., Isaac Muzzy, Caleb Harrington, John Brown, Jedediah Munroe, John Raymond, Nathaniel Wyman, — ten. And the wounded were : — John Robbins, Solomon Peirce, John Tidd, Joseph Comee, Ebenezer Munroe, Jr., Thomas Winship, Nathaniel Farmer, Prince Estabrook, Francis Brown, Jedediah Munroe, — ten. The other towns suffered as follows in their killed and wounded : — *Concord*, none killed, five wounded ; *Acton*, three killed, one wounded ; *Cambridge*, including *Arlington*, six killed, one wounded ; *Needham*, five killed, two wounded ; *Sudbury*, two killed, one wounded ; *Bedford*, one killed, one wounded ; *Woburn*, two killed, three wounded ; *Medford*, two killed ; *Charlestown*, two killed ; *Framingham*, one wounded ; *Dedham*, one killed, one wounded ; *Stow*, one wounded ; *Brookline*, one killed ; *Billerica*, two wounded ;

Chelmsford, two wounded ; *Salem,* one killed ; *Newton,* one wounded ; *Danvers,* seven killed, two wounded ; *Beverly,* one killed, three wounded ; *Lynn,* four killed, two wounded.

It will be seen that Lexington suffered most severely, though some of the towns on the line had three times her population. Next to Lexington, Danvers was the greatest sufferer, though she was one of the most remote towns. The British loss was seventy-three killed, one hundred and seventy-four wounded, and twenty-six missing — mostly taken prisoners.

We stated in the body of the account, that the British officers sent out by Gage on the 18th, probably had their orders to seize Hancock and Adams. If such was the design, the alarm that was given, and the gathering of the minute-men, were amply sufficient to induce them to abandon that design. Hancock and Adams had been at Mr. Clarke's several days, and they remained in his house on the morning of the 19th of April, till some three or four o'clock, when they repaired to the woods on the hill near Mr. Clarke's house, where they could overlook the Common, and they were in a manner witnesses of what occurred on the green till the British left for Concord, when they were conducted to safe quarters in Burlington. It was on the hill here spoken of, that the prophetic spirit of Adams, when he heard the report of the enemy's volley on the Common, broke forth with the joyful exclamation, " *What a glorious morning for America is this.*"

Lexington's patriotic zeal did not subside with the 19th of April. During the siege of Boston she furnished men, fuel and other supplies for the army ; and in the different campaigns to New York, to Ticonderoga, to White Plains, to the Jerseys, to Bennington, to Providence, and other places, she sent, on the shortest notices, her full quota of men ; and in the Continental army she had over one hundred men, who enlisted for three years or during the war. This, for a small town of about seven hundred inhabitants, must be regarded as a liberal supply. And more recently, when the integrity of the Union was assailed by those who had enjoyed its protection and blessings, Lexington furnished, including re-enlistments, two hundred and forty-four men, who readily volunteered to sustain the institutions which our fathers established. Lexington sustained her soldiers liberally, expending $27,000 in the late war. Nearly $2,000 of this was furnished by the ladies, who provided clothing and hospital supplies for the men in the field. But Lexington does not glory in her military achievements alone. She has joyfully cultivated the arts of peace, and has made a respectable advance in civilization. Her population, for reasons already stated, has not advanced rapidly; but her growth has been gradual and healthy. In 1676 the population of the place could not exceed one hundred; in 1776 it probably amounted to seven hundred; and in 1876 to two thousand five hundred and ten. But by the industry of the inhabitants, the wealth of the town has increased in a far greater ratio. We cannot present the taxable value of the property a century ago; but for the last twenty years the town valuation has risen from $1,815,799 to $2,979,711, a gain in twenty years of sixty-four per cent. The number of polls in 1776 was two hundred and three, in 1876, seven hundred and thirty-six. To show the present condition of the town we will state that the number of dwelling houses is 467, the number of horses 473, and the number of cows 1,119.

It has justly been observed that the love of country and the love of learning, are kindred affections and generally go together. As soon as Lexington was incorporated as a town, she erected a school house in the centre of the town, and supported what was generally denominated "a moving school," which was kept in rotation in different sections of the township. During the Revolution no great improvement was made in the cause of education; but in 1795 three additional school houses were erected, and $333 appropriated for the support of schools. This sum was increased from time to time — in 1819 to $900, in 1830 to $1,000, in 1837 to $1,400, in 1850 to $2,400, in 1860 to $3,400, in 1870 to $6,000, in 1875 to $10,100, amounting to $21.72 to each scholar in town between the ages of five and fifteen, and making Lexington No. 10 in the list of three hundred and thirty-eight towns, and No. 6 in the county of fifty-four towns, — a position highly creditable. She has seven good school houses, and supports a High School, with a salary for the teacher of $2,000, being a larger sum than is paid for a High School teacher by any town in the State of the same population, valuation, and number of scholars.

While Lexington has not all the luxuries of the cities and the more wealthy towns, yet she is not behind towns of her population, similarly situated. She has her street lights; and the lamps in her main village and in the public buildings are supplied with gas by a company in the place, which also supplies many of the private families.

She is also favored with a Savings Bank, where her laborers and others, can deposit twice a month, their earnings or any surplus they may have on hand, and thus secure something in prosperity which may serve them in adversity, or enable them to leave something for their families. This institution has been in operation only about five years, and still it has been attended with entire success, and has acquired a permanent character satisfactory to the people.

Like most other towns in the State, Lexington has a variety of religious societies of different denominations — One Unitarian, one Calvinistic, one Baptist, one Union, composed of Unitarians and Universalists, and one Roman Catholic. They all have good houses of worship, — the two first named have houses tastefully finished, — and all are supplied with ministers and have regular preaching. These societies are well sustained.

Not only the churches and school-houses, but the Town Hall is highly creditable to the town. It is a brick building, 95 feet by 58, and 38 feet in height above the basement, with a double Louvre roof, affording an attic hall 14 feet high. This edifice furnishes a large audience hall, apartments for the appropriate town officers, a memorial hall, and library hall. The memorial hall is an octagon, with suitable corridors, containing four niches, filled with four marble life-size statues,—two of soldiers,—one a minute-man of 1775, and the other a Union soldier of 1861. These are consecrated to the *military*, to show our just appreciation of the gallant men by whom our freedom was achieved and has been sustained. The other two niches are filled with the statues of SAMUEL ADAMS and JOHN HANCOCK, the patriot sages who guided public sentiment and animated the zeal of the people, and so prepared the Colonists for self government. The hall also contains tablets with the names of the martyrs of both wars, and bears upon its entrance this appropriate inscription :

LEXINGTON
CONSECRATES THIS HALL AND ITS EMBLEMS
TO THE MEMORY OF THE
FOUNDERS AND THE SUSTAINERS OF OUR FREE INSTITUTIONS.

The library hall is a large, commodious room, appropriately fitted up for the purpose. The library was established in 1868, and now

contains four thousand six hundred volumes, and is constantly
increasing. As its resources furnish about $550 annually, and pub-
lic institutions and private individuals are liberal in their gifts, we
trust that our library, which is free to all, will soon be worthy of the
historic town of Lexington. The library hall also contains many
appropriate relics of the Revolution, and of the men who took part
in the events of that day, such as muskets, swords, powder horns,
and other things too numerous to mention.

The people of Lexington have always felt that they were placed
by Providence in a peculiar position. To be the birth-place of
American liberty, — the spot where the opening scene of the Revolution was laid, where the first blood was shed, the first martyrs fell,
and the first organized resistance made to the king's troops, — has
given to Lexington a historic character, which imposes upon its citizens a sacred regard to the free institutions of the land. And, as
on the morning of the 19th of April, 1775, she met the oppressor
single handed, and was doomed to "tread the wine-press alone," so
she has been able on her commemorative days, to carry forward her
work without the advice or financial aid of her sister towns. In our
Centennial celebration in 1875, we felt constrained to do what we
could to honor the great event which occurred within our borders, a
century ago. While we had no disposition to arrogate to ourselves
any exclusive patriotism, or to impute to others a want of devotion
to their country ; while we were not ambitious to interpolate any
new chapter into our country's annals, to throw other towns into
the shade and thus gain temporarily a false reputation ; we could not
ignore the event of Providence which had, long since, passed into
history, making Lexington the scene of the first encounter, and her
sons the first to confront an oppressor in arms, and to seal their
devotion to freedom with their life blood.

Lexington felt called upon, under these circumstances, to open
wide her doors and to invite the friends of freedom from every part
of the country to meet on her consecrated soil, that we might join
our hearts and our voices in gratitude to the patriots of days gone
by, whose wisdom devised, and whose gallantry achieved our glorious
independence ; and to renew our vows to sustain that independence,
and to make our Republic an example to the world. Our invitations
were sent to the President and suite, to the Governors of all the
States, officers of the army and navy, members of Congress, judges

4

of the Courts, members of our State government, and gentlemen of distinction of every profession in all sections of the country. Nor were our invitations confined to this country. They were sent across the Atlantic, and brought cordial responses from our ministers abroad, and from two distinguished members of the British Parliament. The responses to our invitations were of the most cordial character. We were sensible that we were destined to lead off in a series of Centennial celebrations which, though confined to this country, would exert an influence abroad ; and we resolved that the example we should set should be in harmony with the general designs of these commemorative rejoicings. Nay, without waiting for others, or inquiring into their design or their policy, we, as our fathers did of old, acted on our own judgment ; and knowing that we had a country to harmonize, we extended our invitations to those who had been estranged from us, to show them that we, like the father in the parable, would " meet a great way off," those who had come to themselves and were desirous of returning to the paternal mansion. We intended that all our proceedings should be strictly national, and calculated to heal any disaffection, to remove all distrust, and restore harmony and confidence between different sections of the Union.

Our speakers were selected with reference to this design, and the tone and temper of their speeches were of a patriotic and conciliatory character ; and while we have witnessed with pleasure the tone of later celebrations and the voice of the press, we can congratulate ourselves that this fraternal, forgiving spirit was first uttered in Lexington ; that we were permitted to be the harbingers of that returning harmony so important to the prosperity of the country. And we flatter ourselves that the report which went forth from Lexington Common in 1875, like the report from the same place in 1775, may have contributed to the production of confidence between the North and the South.

The attendance at our celebration greatly exceeded our expectation. The President and his Cabinet, and distinguished guests from every section of the country honored us by their presence, and the legion — for they were many — flocked to our town, and so blocked our roads that they were for a great part of the day impassable. It was estimated by the best judges that there were in the town that day, at least a hundred thousand people. Such numbers disappointed many of our guests, and greatly mortified us, because we could not accommodate them as we desired. But on further reflection we, and we believe most of our guests who were incommoded, rejoice rather than otherwise, that the crowd was so great. This gathering by thousands showed that the spirit of 1775 was not extinct. And we perceived that the mere story of the 19th of April, '75, had produced such a ground-swell of patriotism, such a feeling of gratitude to our Revolutionary fathers, and such a sense of the worth of our institutions, as would ensure the perpetuity of the Republic. Thus our disappointment was turned into rejoicing.

CITIZENS OF LEXINGTON, the approaching Fourth of July is the anniversary of the declaration of the nation's independence — the announcement in Philadelphia on the Fourth of July, 1776, of a fact which practically occurred in Lexington on the 19th of April, 1775. But the event itself is important, and the Centennial anniversary is a suitable time to recount our past blessings, to review our history, and form plans for such improvement as may redound to the honor of the country. But above all things, we must remember that righteousness exalteth a nation, and that our country's prosperity depends upon justice, temperance, and the great principles of moral rectitude and integrity — principles on which our institutions were founded. If we have departed from them, let us return to them as to the ark of our safety, and recognize our dependence upon Him who rules the nations of the earth. This reform is greatly needed to save our national character, and no time and place are more suitable to commence this reform than this Centennial, and the place where our freedom had its birth. The time and the place being propitious, we should consecrate ourselves to the great cause of national morality, and trust to the sacred guidance of Him on whom our fathers placed their reliance. Yes :

> " Here upon this sacred sod,
> The children of the free,
> Who follow where our fathers trod,
> Must learn to trust our fathers' God,
> The God of Liberty."

At the close of the eighteenth century the fame of Lexington was so fully appreciated by the State, that the Legislature made an appropriation, " For the purpose of erecting in said town a Monument of Stone, on which shall be engraved the names of the eight men, inhabitants of Lexington, who were slain on the morning of the 19th of April, 1775, by a party of British troops ; together with such other inscription as, in the judgment of the Selectmen and the approbation of the Governor and Council, shall be calculated *to preserve to posterity a record of the first effort made by the people of America for the establishment of their freedom and independence.*"

The inscription upon the Monument was furnished by the patriotic Mr. Clarke, and met the approbation of the Governor and Council. It is so replete with devotion to the cause of America, and the love of freedom and the rights of mankind, and so true to history and the spirit of the day, that we will give it entire :

SACRED TO LIBERTY AND THE RIGHTS OF MANKIND!!!
THE FREEDOM AND INDEPENDENCE OF AMERICA,
SEALED AND DEFENDED WITH THE BLOOD OF HER SONS.

This Monument is erected
By the inhabitants of Lexington,
Under the patronage and at the expense of
The Commonwealth of Massachusetts,
To the memory of their fellow Citizens,
Ensign *Robert Munroe*, and Messrs. *Jonas Parker*,
Samuel Hadley, *Jonathan Harrington*, *Jun.*,
Isaac Muzzy, *Caleb Harrington*, and *John Brown*,
Of Lexington, and *Asahel Porter* of Woburn,
Who fell on the Field the First Victims to the
Sword of British Tyranny and oppression,
On the Morning of the ever memorable
Nineteenth of April An. Dom. 1775.
The Die was cast!!!
The Blood of these Martyrs
In the cause of God and their country
Was the Cement of the Union of these States, then
Colonies, and gave the Spring to the Spirit, Firmness
And Resolution of their Fellow Citizens.
They rose as one Man to revenge their Brethren's
Blood, and at the point of the sword to assert and
Defend their native Rights.
They nobly dared to be free!!
The contest was long, bloody and affecting,
Righteous Heaven approved the solemn appeal,
Victory crowned their arms ; and
The Peace, Liberty and Independence of the United
States of America was their Glorious Reward.

1775

1861

SAM'L. ADAMS

JOHN HANCOCK.

www.ingramcontent.com/pod-product-compliance
Lightning Source LLC
Chambersburg PA
CBHW032143080426
42733CB00008B/1187